Henry C. Finney

FIRE GATE POEMS

A Journey of Spiritual Healing

Poems, Paintings & Graphic Art

iUniverse, Inc.
Bloomington

Fire Gate Poems
A Journey of Spiritual Healing

iUniverse books may be ordered through booksellers or by contacting:

iUniverse
1663 Liberty Drive
Bloomington, IN 47403
www.iuniverse.com
1-800-Authors (1-800-288-4677)

ISBN: 978-1-4620-3674-5 (sc)
ISBN: 978-1-4620-3676-9 (hc)
ISBN: 978-1-4620-3675-2 (e)

Printed in the United States of America

iUniverse rev. date: 10/14/2011

Fire Gate

house in flames
enter the fire gate
to come home

Figure 1: "Tree Line," Oil on Linen, 24" x 30," 1990.

In memory of

Christopher Anson Finney

1970 – 2000

Preface

These poems commemorate the death, by his own hand, of my only son, Christopher Anson Finney. They do not trace my exact route through the land of grief I then traversed, so much as they express my moods before, during and after the trek to healing. While initially grim, the journey has ended in wonder, and sometimes joy. I don't know how or why I've been blessed by such a transformation, except to say that it was made possible by entering what I call "the fire gate" of my grief—hence the reference in the book's title. That is to say, I was able to heal by honestly facing and experiencing the wrenching emotions of loss.

The images that accompany the poems were all, with the sole exception of a painting by my father, created by me. As will be seen, they include sketches, drawings, photographs, paintings, and various types of fine-art prints. They were all selected and digitally edited for their legibility in black-and-white. The originals of most of the paintings and pastels are in color. Except for the raven-poem image, particular graphics and poems were not created specifically for each other. Rather, the images were selected and placed on the basis of what felt to me like their resonance with the poems they accompany. They are not "illustrations" in the usual sense, so much as "evocations."

It is the poems that form the book's structure. Because the transformation has indeed been a personal journey, they are grouped to express or echo my experiences during that journey. They begin with "Origins," touching on a wide range of moods and memories from various times before the tragedy. The poems of shock and grief follow in "Abyss." The remaining three groups document my rebirth, beginning with poems of "Return," followed next by poems of "Renewal," and concluding with some expressions of "Wonder."

Such an arrangement, however, should be understood as being metaphorical as much as literal; the poems are not necessarily presented in the sequence of their writing. I have found that life is just not like that; it does not unfold in a strictly linear manner. It is more like a kaleidoscopic light show that has a temporal sequence, but whose shapes and colors often appear jumbled and even repetitive as the show unfolds. Passionate reds, tranquil blues and ominous darks reappear throughout, but in an ever-changing array. In short, the temporal ordering of the poems is not exact.

The poems reflect a process of healing, but not in the simplistic sense of having returned to the way life was before my son died. My life was forever changed by that shot in the Arizona desert where he fell. As is so often true in peoples' lives, it seems, the transformation that followed was not entirely of my own choosing. Rather, I was thrust into it. My only choice was either to die with him or to search for rebirth. After a long struggle, I chose the latter, with the result that my experience of the world is deeper and richer now than it ever was before—even if rather more sensitive to pain. May those who read these poems and view their accompanying images experience something of the same blessings themselves.

I should note, finally, that because some names and references may be unfamiliar to many readers, brief explanations are provided in the "Uncommon Names and References" section at the end of the book.

Contents

Origins

Figure 2: Portrait of the Artist's
Father, Ross Lee Finney, charcoal and
digitized music score, 12" x 9," 1980.

Childhood Dreams

For years
I sensed
my childhood dreams
were omens.

They echoed
as I went to sleep
a yearning for
my father's music
from his piano through the wall.

I long believed that
dreams, like Fates, spun
life's threads
thin strands of necessity

requiring that someday...
I couldn't tell.

They even revealed death
bolting me awake
falling
terrified
into the ink of night.

But, now grown
choices made
father long since gone
I know
omens are only passing dreams
and death is just
the fading sound of wind
in yellow fall aspens.

Figure 3: "Self-Portrait," india
ink, 12.5" x 9.5," 1980.

Wintry Edge

White trail blue
shadows surge
pulsing
each thrust and glide.

What force
drives
heart and lungs
pounding
lunging
to the edge?

By skiing harder
I will become
one
of these bent pines
heaped with snow.

Wispy chunks fall away
Pine rosin scent fresh.
I disappear.
Years slip by.

Then
eyes tingling with salt
breath begins to fail
the wintry edge recedes.

The pines slip quietly away
awaiting my return.

Figure 4: "Seashore Rocks," charcoal, 17" x 13.5," 1983.

Foundation

safe, secure, heels dry-printing
rings on hard sand
wandering through foam tongues
breakers
thundering
endlessly rolling in
white roar filling the haze

churning cascades mesmerize
crash after crash
merging
drawn in
will dissolving

foam swirls past
stones loosen under foot

suddenly, unawares
a bone-jarring thump
into clattering gravel
and a vigorous salty swim

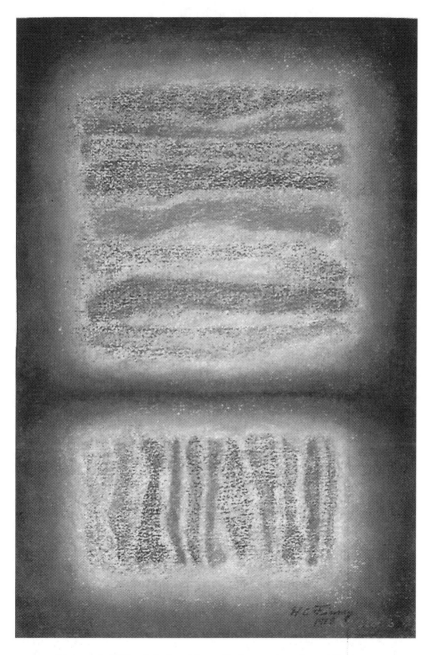

Figure 5: "Way Marker No. 3," charcoal, 21" x 14," 1988.

Silver Morning

I am a Charioteer.
I thunder horrific frays
not knowing
frenzied
blood on my lips
dumb to the slaughter.

I lash the reins, driving hard.
The oracle guides
my thrashing horses.

Faint dawn illuminates
red dust clouds.
My havoc war machine
runs down unseen foes
who fall beneath
maimed or slain.

Then
amidst the hellish war
thin light creeps forth.
Voices fragment.
The din
the dust
the clang of battle
fade.

Senses drugged
dull to dawn
I stumble through
the dark river.
Deafened
gaunt
my blood-lust ebbs.
Memory drains away.

My senses slowly rising
a blurred jay flickers
just above
the mirror-surface pond of sleep.
Faint stripes of blue unfurl.

Birdsong returns
dissolving
the madness of night
into cool silver morning.

Figure 6: "Basho Pond," 35mm color photograph, 1987.

Ocean Games

We walk the ocean sand for hours
unhurried
feeling the moist air
hearing the salt flume.

Thundering surf whitens the world
crash after crash
merging
until their progeny
energy spent
lap foam tongues around our feet.

Children run after receding washes
to plunge
their sticks yet further in
then scream as they race back
to escape the next wave's ominous assault.

Alert to impending defeat
reading all the sea's signs to predict my range
I tread the edge of each new fan
knowing any misjudgment
will force retreat.
With a thrill, I gauge the entire sea
comprehending it all for my intended victory
until
unreckoned flood rushing in
I give hasty ground.

Tiny birds, legs strumming
invisibly
rush each ebb
to feed in measured flurry

then scurry back
—droll unison flock—
from the closing foamy attack.
An unexpected surge chases them to flight.
Unruffled, they return.

Instinctively we dance
with forces of our destruction.
We toy with fate.
Through our games we merge, a moment
with the sea
with sand, foam, wind
white sound

until
thunder fading
games ceaseless even in our absence
we forsake the dissolving border zone
and return to roads we know.

Figure 7: "Monterey Surf," 35mm color photograph, 1997.

Leaving Home

What is this sandy home
we labor on for years
a great fortress built
amid the salty scent of ocean air
where circling sea birds cry?

only to find
in weary resignation
the remorseless ebb
eroding its foundations?

Aging, grown weak
we grab
flailing
balance lost
at illusions of achievement.

Words trail off.
We collect symbols of past loves
like your warbling caged canary.
We cling to fragments of mind
that shaped our pride
and very definition.

Only to awaken one morning
like you
spent
songbird clutched in your hands
blood on its beak
crushed by grief and fear.

Exhausted
our bowels begin their return to the earth.
Life and body ebb.
We forget to listen
to rain pattering
on welcome waiting leaves.

A warm hand may hold ours as we drift away.
Did you feel it when your heart faded
too tired to listen any more?

Figure 8: "El Castillo del Rey (Tulum)," india ink, 9" x 11," 1988.

Alas

I want to go where good friends linger
to write a poem of sorrow
in a room
where we brothers went
to play and laugh and build
a model plane
that, when tested, came to ruin.

But no one's there.
Dust floats in the sunlight.
Too late.
He left to write
a book of dollars without me.
I write my poem alone.
He hardly recognizes me now, alas.

Figure 9: My Older Brother, Ross L. Finney,
35mm color photograph, 1998.

Figure 10: Me and My Older Brother, photographed
by my father, 1938, in Menton, France.

Large As an Egg

I have come, it would seem
to visit his cancer
large as an egg.
He knows it's there.
He alternates between
fear and a dreamy look.
It glows in his abdomen.
He tastes dread in his mouth.

When the phone rings
He's in command again.
"No, revision is not needed."
"Yes, I'll mail it tomorrow."
Afterwards, he seems distracted.

He's forgotten
how seagulls cry
how the taste of chocolate
surpasses knowing.

Desperation.
Shrink the egg in vinegar
take herbs
eat hormones
to restore lost hope.

"We will buy a door today," he says
to be installed, he says
by migrant workers.
"I'll call the lawyer on Monday"
to update his will, he says.
Not much to the kids, though,
hooked on anger and achievement.
Most goes to the Dharma Center

one family replacing another.

We hug now
vital as red meat.
Then his too-long laugh
clouds his eyes
like opaque green garden pools.

I say, "Let's visit the sea."
He says, "I will schedule meetings."
I say, "There is haze in the air."
He says, "I'll go over her head, the bitch."

It is raining.
Somewhere near
the drops become
a water metronome.

Sadly I await.
I can hardly hear him anymore.
The spicy taste of chai lingers
around my tongue.
Soft rain patters on the glass.

Figure 11: "Pacific Grove Surf," charcoal, 14" x 17," 1994.

Flight

For Ross, 1933 – 2000

Dear brother, as you turn the gate
know Emptiness as not just void
but boundlessness where all rejoins
the flowing river of our fate;
where lives arise and fade per chance;
where Shiva and the Ancients dance.

Your labors' gifts will live on long
like generations of a song;
and now, as payment in reverse
your breath blends with the universe.

From teachers' love and radiant dreams
of golden Gods and wars foreseen
of benefactions and release
from karmic bonds and on to peace
you've glimpsed their mysteries past the door
and know your Buddha Mind will soar.

So, when your fledging moment comes
don't hesitate nor judge the height
but let your Lama teacher nudge
you into endless flight.

Figure 12: "Stump Abstraction," from 35mm color photograph," 1992.

Abyss

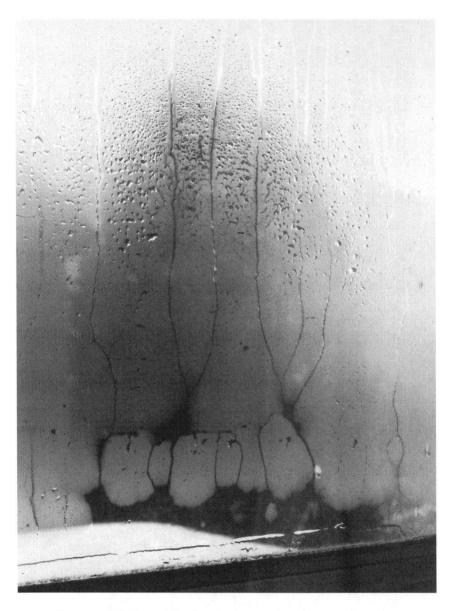

Figure 13: "Winter Window," 35mm color photograph, 1988.

Moon-Faced Buddha: A Requiem

I.

driving down
the morning mesa
sometime then
in a micro-second
the mountain exploded

II.

(Sing softly…)
rock-a-bye baby in the tree top
when the wind blows, your cradle will rock
when your bough breaks
the cradle will fall
and down will come Christopher
cradle and all

III.

we learned
officer knocking
that evening, late
he thrust
an iron poker in my chest
I remember the color red
stinging eyes

IV.

(chant slowly…)
Christopher Anson sat on a wall
Christopher Anson had a great fall
both of his parents and all of his friends
couldn't put Anson together again

V.

Carl
your cat
six toes each foot
asleep
paws twitch
dreams
where you are

VI.

(Sing softly…)
mother put the kettle on
father put the kettle on
sister put the kettle on
just three for tea

VII.

every afternoon
sun heats your ashes
at night
holly leaves scratch
our window

VIII.

(Chant sing-song…)
ring around the rosie
pocket full of posies
Christopher is ashes
all fall *down*

IX.

you planted my garden
hoed my life
grew secrets we never learned
you were in love

X.

(chant softly…)
Chris isn't hot
Chris isn't cold
Christopher's in a box
thirty years old

XI.

meditate
still point
breathing
you in
night stars
twinkling

XII.

sun-faced Buddha
Buddha of life
moon-faced Buddha
Buddha of death

Figure 14: My son Christopher, 35mm color photograph," 1996.

Figure 15: "Dragon Fly," india ink, 6" x 6," 1979.

On River Avon

Groping, I dream
my first life recollection
on sparkling River Avon.

But afflicted memory transforms
the stream to River Styx.
Christopher, my son, lying
upon his gurney
somehow rises from his
vinyl body bag of death.

Now we sit
weightless
on a sunny row boat seat.

He sits with me on River Avon.
He cannot speak, lips
sealed by a crusty line of white.
Sun twinkles a water dance.

We drift, dreaming. Suddenly
a concussive blast.
He slumps.
From his temple
a bullet spews
brains and blood.
His body settles.

Holding his limp hand
I look.
His face blooms
colors of dead fruit
oranges
reds of cherries and
purple plums
green melons
awful ochers
blacks and brown earths.

We float, drift on.
Elms over-arch the river.
Christopher leans near
revealing what the vinyl body sheath
had hid
the autopsy
the swollen galls of fluid
the hemorrhages
the butchered thoracic slit
sewn back in place
with sinews.

A zephyr drifts us further out
the ocean mouth in view now.
I see his dull starched hair straight-
    combed back.
The multi-colors of his dead flesh
flutter
a languid butterfly
pulsing to some higher
air and calm.

Ripples murmer.
I do not know how long
we drift.
A grassy edge of bank approaches
grows larger and
we bump.
Releasing his dead hand
I rise and step ashore
alone.

He slumps forward now
Shows no signs
of my dream, my exit.
His funerary shell drifts out to sea
to his origins
where I cannot dream
the pains he has endured.

Figure 16: "Pine Bough," india ink, notebook sketch, 1988.

Fire Tiger

Stars grieve his cold body
his face
a battered rainbow
body hollow
consigned to burn.

The fire tiger
smelling blood
kills all hope.
He gnaws the carcass
licks the ashes.

Dumb animals, mouths empty
somehow know
the reality of death.
They hesitate
look back a final time
then wander off
alone.

From a triple
brilliant belt
death at hand
Orion draws his sword.

The Fire Tiger, now in fierce embrace
devours all desire.

Blinded
appetite gone
I too wander off
alone.

Figure 17: "Fire," monoprint, 13.5" x 11," 1998.

Figure 18: "Leaf," india ink, notebook sketch, 1988.

Last Sounds

I never felt as sick
as when sounds
faded and nausea
transformed
flesh to fire.

I never felt as sick as when
dumb I could only
stare rolling
lights flashing slide by
and my bones feel
the rhythm of
throbbing tires.

So sick that
chaotic time convened
a garish night of ghosts
spasmodic lights
of Halloween white strobes
flashing reds.

Pain took charge.
A pale tiger
gnawed my bones.
Vision faded.

explosions of silver
plasma flesh
deep needles
eyes stinging wet
burning gristle smell

The stunted man nearby
moaned
"help me, someone!"
But no help came
because his deformity
and my pain
could not be treated
    seen
        or categorized.

I am reduced
to networks and cells.

I never felt as sick as when
knowledge drained away
releasing me to slip
into unknowing.

Longing for solitude
I crawled off
an animal
to lie beneath medicinal plants.
Chirruping insects infused
the dusk of late summer eves.

And a whisper counseled
"Just keep going…
just hear
the world's last sounds."

Figure 19: "Uinta Mountain Cliff," charcoal, 19" x 24," 1979.

Figure 20: "Totem," lithograph, 15.5" x 15.5," 1994.

Netherworld

I. Fire

My son's self-execution has led me
to a charcoal netherworld
ominous with signs and demons
hot
an abyss of sorrow that
corrodes my soul.

My throat constricts.
I rock hopeless
head in hands
to weep for days.
My mouth is salt.

The deepest grief is in
the muscles, the inner organs.
The seizures
start there, moving
upward, throbbing
a pressure in the blood
that deadens the nerves
leaving my body drained.

It is twilight.
Spent
I slip into morphine sleep.

Dark dawn is a dangerous time.
I only wake to mourn again.
The larynx cramps.
Glands under my tongue ache.
Stretching dumbly out
I flex and clench hands.
Groping, they vent spasms
futile jerky finger movements.

"Eka, show me your grief
and I will put it to rest for you,"
said the Chinese patriarch of Zen.
Alas, the reply:
"I've searched everywhere;
my grief is nowhere to be found."

I too search
to somehow grasp the sadness.
But grief is not a thing.
Instead, it is like breathing in
the acrid-smelling smoke of wild fire.

II. Water

An ancient adept asked
"since grief— past, present and future—
cannot be grasped
tell me
from whence come these tears?"

No one knows.
Grief can only be voiced.
When joyous, sing.
When stricken, cry.

"Let tears run down like a river
day and night. Give thyself no rest;
let not the apple of thine eye cease."
(Lamentations 2:18)

Grief is a grisly addiction
born of disemboweled desire.
My son? A desire?
Like Eka, I will cut my arm for Bodhidharma
if that will raise the dead.

But alas
I sense only
the howling immediacy of now.

The scene changes.
I am tumbling
yearning toward death.

Seated now on a pier's end
legs dangling
black water flickers oblivion.
I am saved only by
a whisper of wings.

The nightmare shifts again.
A room with concrete walls.
No exit.
Hard wooden beds.
Wails of the damned.
I have become the Goddess
Kwan Yin
hearing all the world's cries.

We cry together
a house of yearning ghosts
of exotic birds.
We mourn together.
We are the world.

How can the secret have been kept so well?

Our bitter ordination to the rites
reveals the truth that rivers everywhere display
that flowing taste so clear and sweet by day
then turn to salt from world's tears at night.

Figure 21: "Organic Forms Still Life," charcoal, 18" x 23," 1989.

Mother and Child

A child shrieks in the black of night.
Who now will hold the mother?

Return

Figure 22: "Vergennes," dry color pastel, 19" x 25," 1988.

The Lives of Grasses

Recovering from my deep frozen winter
I wander now
amid a sea of grasses
of new-grown wild flowers
where just last week
(I've lost track)
snow lay deep.

No path remains.

Despite your absence
summer has secretly returned.
No pretending winter losses any more.
I re-awaken
like this field
whose sea of waving tassels
swishing, aromatic

beckoning savory awareness
bids me to remember
a primeval gratitude for
the lives of grasses.

I re-affirm, re-enter
my neglected garden
step through grassy clumps
inhale fragrances from the East.

Once
years before
to service coming campers
machines broken
I tried to mow a great grass field
with clippers.
Overwhelmed by impossibility
I was reduced
to solitary snips.
One snip. Another snip. Then the next
swallowed by the boundless field.

Will dissolving
hope gone
I found this endless clipping
by some miracle
(snow now forgotten)
brought warm release
saved me
when my trance was slowly permeated
by distant throbbing motor sounds.

By then I was delirious
with the scent of mown grasses
each clip, each snip
nudging open a gateless gate
to this Now.

Figure 23: "Barlow's Field," dry color pastel, 12.5" x 12.5," 1988.

Figure 24: "Flowers," dry color pastel, 25" x 19," 1988.

Figure 25: "23 Bank Street," watercolor, 15" x 22," 1983.

Strange Angel

Peering down
over the building cornice
I see a crowd milling in the city street below.
They are waiting.
On the rooftop, where I stand
another crowd awaits, as well
hesitant, milling, uncertain
looking silently about
for some cue, some direction.

Something stirs below—
an airy whirring sound ascending.
Turning, I see, just beyond the cornice, rise
from street below a glowing apparition
a most strange angel
floating upwards.

Above our heads now, in full command

he begins to lead a dance.
Hovering wings outstretched, clear-eyed
smiling softly
my luminous dead son begins
to lead us on a path
to full release
from grief to joy, to celebration.

Murmurs sweep
the expectant, milling crowds.
A few and I begin to sway. Others join
and soon
faces smiling now
the crowd lets go. Singing
we soon become the voice
of this strange angel.

Cerulean sky back-lights my spectral son
the exotic angel, who hovers
wings aglow, and joins
our blooming happiness, inspiring
all of us to dance.

The ones below join in, for they can
see the angel too, and hear the song.
All have been awaiting this release.
We form a festival of faces laughing now.
We are reborn, singing
inspired by
this odd evangelist
my resurrected son.

Figure 26: "Barranca No. 1," oil on canvas, 30" x 30," 1995.

Figure 27: "Family Portrait"—daughter Catherine, me and my wife Helen in Chile, digital color image, 2002.

Family Time

I sit motionless.
With windows, doors, thresholds open
the great room fire crackles
suffusing piñon incense smells.

Spirits and demons visit.
They whisper
telling secrets and tales
of gods and hungry ghosts.

Some linger, yearning
sharing regrets, desires, fears.
I listen gratefully to their stories.

I serve tea.
It is a family time.

Figure 28: "Woods," charcoal, 14" x 17," 1998.

Figure 29: "Flowers," by my father, Ross Lee Finney, oil on linen, 16" x 13," circa 1955.

Glowing Red

Let me tell you about the time
it never stopped raining
the time my memories washed away
in roiling flood.

There had been signs—
sleeping all day
forgetting to shave
arriving late
speaking too softly because
there seemed no point.

Flowers didn't bloom that spring.
It was the year my father died
in a public home
where blue paint chips hung
where nurses smiled and walked away
assuming he was deaf.

It just rained and rained
until
one morning
the sun
after enlightening
eastern mythic lands
warmed the great ocean and
returned full cleansed
glowing red on my adobe wall.

Figure 30: "Portrait of the Artist's Father," Ross Lee
Finney, dry color pastel, 20" x 17," 1986.

Guardians

Night times I wander
a dim world between dreams
and protocols of day
searching. Sometimes

across glittering rivulets
I see dragons
guardians of times
past and future
sparkling gold and blue.

They beckon and say
"Do you want to know the truth?
Do you want to know, again
the possibility of choice?
that soaring long forgotten?

Yes?
Then come close.
We are your hopes
nightmares
yearnings.
We are the moist, musty earth
the fire colors of autumn
creators of streams
bearers of life, your life, now.
If you want rebirth, come closer."

Surrounded now, I see their scales
glinting blue and gold
my entire life in their lucent eyes.
Milling near, they comfort
my frightened reasons
cut away my understandings
like useless underbrush.

They say
"Who are you now, with all your knowledge
      gone?
You don't know? Of course not.
We will guide you to
your most luminous visions
your original life
before you were born."

Figure 31: "Johnson Woods, Stream," india ink, 8" x 11," 1986.

Figure 32: "Vermont Woods," india ink, 10" x 7," 1986.

The Moment Before Birth

Alive with the knowledge of death
this predawn hour
frog chorus chirruping
on, and off
the reptilian root of my brain
buzzes with lost memories.

I drift in the constellations.

Night's last hour is when
I walk with the dead
look into the mystery of fire
and know the stirrings of life
the moment before birth.

Gradually, despite my desire to linger
the ether where everything originates
dissolves into the freshness of dawn
into daytime awareness
where predawn memories are weakened by light
like the fading of sun-bleached cloth.

If only I could grasp
the seed of my dark churning sun.
All my urgent questions arise there
in the faint glow before dawn.

Why the endless suffering?
the pain?

Yearning.
Desire.
They start here with the question
"Who am I?"
It is my way of filling the void
glimpsed just before dawn.

As the dead fade away
fear and desire fill
my heart, blood pulsing.

That is why, during the day
I walk so far
always asking
"What is next?" and
"Shall I like
or dislike what I do?"

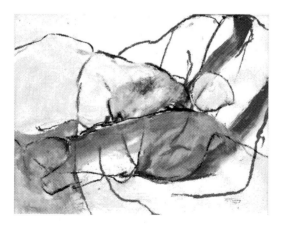

Figure 33: "Reclining Figures," color gouache
and oil stick, 14" x 19.5," 1991.

Figure 34: "Open Figure Gesture," color gouache, 29" x 24," 1991.

Farewell

At last
after years of darkness
everywhere I hear the rustle of cottonwood
leaves fluttering in the sun;
and in their midst
my dead mother and father quietly converse.

Figure 35: "Portrait of the Artist's Mother," Gretchen Ludke Finney, charcoal, 16" x 11," 1981.

Figure 36: "Portrait of the Artist's Father," charcoal, 17" x 11," 1982.

The Price of Admission

shattered glass
ravaged families
overcrowded morgues
lost ego empire wars

no end to violence
to suffering
like incurable cancer
searing, nauseous
pain everywhere

well, get used to it
there's no promise of improvement
oh, we can hope
we can love
but we just as often lapse
back
into greed, hate, violence

and nothing lasts

still
some happy moments pass
like silver starbursts
in silver streams
and even amidst ruin
children play tag

we're born human
live briefly
search for answers

often falsely trusting
there'll be time
breathe each next new moment
feel our grief
and the suffering of others, perchance
the grief shared
in our communal gilded lobby

and we may wonder why we love and kill
and ponder how rose luck blooms
and wilts
and how our sobbing and salt tears
our guffaws and gay laughter
in their golden turns are
simply the price of admission

Figure 37: "Burst," lithograph, 10" x 7," 1992.

Renewal

Figure 38: "The Lives of Grasses," pencil notebook sketch, 1986.

Wild Flower

...Just as firewood does not become firewood again
  after it is ash,
so after one's death, one does not return to life again.
Life is a period of itself.
Death is a period of itself...
They are like winter and spring.

Zen Master Eihei Dogen
Shobogenzo Genjo Koan, 1233

you just called me "wild flower"

odd

I never think about it

just dancing summer hot
prairie wind
this undulating field
no pondering
life or death
spring or fall

but since you wax so eloquent
I must tell you
I can't bear long conversations
praises
taxonomies
or bouquets

teach you?
yes, I will teach you

listen

I know the slow birth and death of seasons
summer's tongues turn
silent
gusty chill late fall
I wither
sporadic cold
flurries now
covered mute by snow

coming—a crown of yellow petals around
an umber sun
going— a ragged black twig in snow

but do not make too much
of coming and going
I appear again in spring
you must understand
my death is
simply
a frozen period of itself

just as my summer life is
a green and golden period of itself
   separate
      sequential
        quite proper
my cycle of unending changes

now
let me be
when you return
late spring first blossoming perhaps
we can continue with
the Teachings.

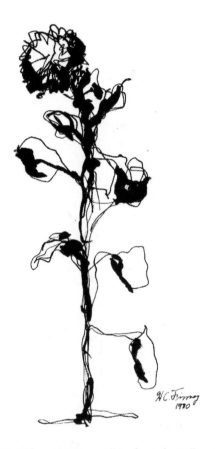

Figure 39: "Flower Gesture," india ink, 10" x 5," 1981.

Figure 40: "Tree Gesture," pencil, 15" x 14." 1979.

Small Blessings

Day after day
grief and tears
laughing
sweating sore
muscles
cell hunger
wolfing
eggs and potatoes.
What a drag!
What a joy!

Figure 41: "Raven Dies and Returns to Talk," detail, mixed media and gold leaf on canvas, 50" x 38," (detail 23" x 38"), 2006.

Raven Dies and Returns to Talk

> I shan't die, I shan't go anywhere,
> I'll be here;
> But don't ask me anything;
> I shan't answer.
>
> Ikkyu, 15th C.

Raven lay feather-matted in roadside grass
residue of some swift unseen violence
neck twisted, one eye forever open.
I brought him home to hear his stories.

He came in the night.
He stole meat and fled.
He slept with our children
hopped away on one foot
right wing unfurled.

He speaks in clicks from dead treetops
posturing
mimicking
for pure fun.

Raven told how
one night
he brought the sun.
"Ha, ha," he clacked, story spun,
"You'll believe anything I say."

"If I fly to the mountain
call fading
How will you survive the night
not knowing
when it draws close
whose ghost you hear?"

"Like you, we live in pairs
and talk endlessly."

"Unlike you, we know enough
to sleep in large groups."

Raven slept
night stars
deep cold
dark silhouettes
no sign of dawn

"The days are easy.
Why do you have such trouble?
When I fly, I go here and there.
When I call, there is only voice.
When I eat, I just tear the flesh.
That's all."

His skull is bare now.
He hasn't moved for over a year.
If I speak, he still hears
and answers with silence.

Figure 42: "Mt. Mansfield," dry color pastel, 18.5" x 24.5," 1987.

Ode to Basalt

Viscous and angry with stupendous heat
I extrude through cracks and fissures
glowing
crawling
boiling ocean surges with a vacuous hiss
grunting pillows from the
mountain's core.

Through a ragged portal I escape
to celebrate fire
run a glowing river.
Smelling of acrid sulfur
I spatter the earth with
abrasive nettles that tear flesh.

My body petrifies
a sea of bubbles
interstices of crystals.
I am a jewel.

What languid lava remains
cools
slowly
forming calm columnar hexagons.

As the great plates move
during my late summers years
I crumble
become earth
nourish the world.

Sheltering in cracks and vacuoles
plants take root
creatures hide.
I shield them.
I am their mother.

And you are my most passionate lover.
How you yearn to come inside
mingling with hexagons
to celebrate eternity with me.

Figure 43: "Basalt Crystal," 35mm color photograph, 2000.

Night Pond

Coming and going, I am wet with rain.
Leave for a different place. No drier.
So I return.
Walking, I stop, then walk again.
More sitting. Warm sun.
Wandering now, going out, to something better, maybe?
No better. More sitting. Belly rises, falls.
Then more walking. Aching knees.
Slow paces this time.
Maybe it will be different. It isn't.
In. Out. Back again.
Feeling deeply tired.
Lie down to sleep
roll over, then the other way.
Jangling wakeup bell.
Water on the face, then more sitting.
At breakfast now.
Chew, swallow, get up, wash dishes.
Hot tea with sugar.
Come back; then go again.
Into what? Out from where?. I blink. Don't know.
That itch again. Scratch.
Standing once more, then walking—always
from here to there and back.
Sit. Sleep. Arise. Bright sunrise. Non-thinking.
No striving. Reborn.
One day, sitting, thoughts wander off, dissolve.
Breezes and soft rains come.
One day, mind transcends itself to utter stillness.
Calm. Deep peace.
Like a full moon mirrored on a dark night pond.

Figure 44: "Pond Space," dry color pastel, 11" x 23.5," 1990.

Figure 45: "Barranca Study No. 3," color gouache, 5.5" x 7.5," 1996.

Live Ruins

I walk the tawny canyon
air pungent with leaf smells and grasses
searching ancient doors.
They appear in canyon walls
through waves of heat
pueblo T's of truth
offering
cool moments
centuries of murmuring.

Across the creek, now a trickle
giant cottonwoods
tell stories.
Shriveled leaves float yellow to the earth.

Whose voices do I hear?

Rustling.

The earth ruins are warm.
Cottonwood trunks infused with pinkish greens
sway like long ago.
Lacy branches splay
a cobalt sky
release surging whispers
of families long dead.

Hints of sage-green yellows
glow just beyond the heat field
on the hill behind
where children played
chased rabbits.

Now, each day's sunlight retells their stories.

The grasses and scrub oaks had names then too.
The sky breathed then as now.
They're all still here.

The languid moment knows me and asks
what part I play.
It always answers, "I know, I know."

Figure 46: "Cottonwoods," dry color pastel, 17" x 14," 1995.

Figure 47: "Temporal Canyon Veil," 35mm color photograph, 1995.

Cycles

I awake during the day
sleep at night.

The transitions are difficult.

Still lost in dim mazes of sleep
stumbling upon bones of old friends
early dawn in this solitary place
is a time heavy with ghosts and demons.

Then, slowly enveloping the trees
sunlight returns.

During the day, I paint.
Some of my canvases glow and sing;
others refuse their favors
remain mute.

Then again
late in the afternoon of this live-oak winter
life drains away
leaving cotton mists
a faint glint from some distant vineyard.

Gradually, darkness arises
like vapor from the earth.
My friend the owl comes to hoot.

During the night, endless, unconscious, nameless
I fend off madness with red coals
return to my origins
hear the stars sing.

It is our cycle, laughing and crying
exulting in the rediscovery of colors
grieving for lost times.
I forget even to ask who I am.

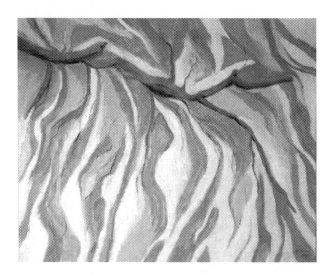

Figure 48: "Canyon Veil," oil on linen, 40" x 50," 2008.

Figure 49: "Witness," photo-etching and aquatint,
from a 1966 drawing, 16.5" x 13.5," 1992.

Wonder

Figure 50: "Nude Gesture," pencil, 12" x 9," 1991.

Lost Page From a Book of Hours

Give these devotions no appointed hour.
Do them between, unplanned
at odd times of day.

After each bell's resonance dissolves
listen intently for a faint melody
and then wait. Patiently wait. You will know.

But don't expect sudden transformation
that you can measure, like
a birthday party with dancing.
That comes much later, for some.

"Ten thousand years under the ice,"
moaned Zen Master Hakuin
crouching all the while
a big cat hungry for dinner.

But dancing, yes, yes!
No need to wait!
Clap your hands.
Dance any time.
You don't need a party or
a book of hours.

Do it between
appointed holy times
like when you hear
rustling aspens, or
the broad-leaf patter of rain.

Figure 51: "Calligraphic Gesture," india ink, 30" x 22," 1991.

Figure 52: "Embracing Figures,"
color monoprint,13.5" x 11," 1998.

Home

I am going home
not to my house
from here to there
but to where pine needles
crunch under foot.

I could go somewhere else
hopes invested in some great aspiration
but I can already taste apples and cinnamon
so why bother?

At home everything passes through me—
hollow raven croak
hot sun pine rosin smell
oak leaves clattering
helicopter far overhead
rotor heart thumping.

Home is my hot sun shadow walking.

Home is where our skins touch
moist
no future.
It is where we lie
in soothing warm
volcanic pools.

I am spring.
Fields glow yellow-green
beneath the mountain.
More rain is on the way.

I am giddy with discovery
that, unbeknownst to me before
—so busy in my search—
this lucid moment home
is everywhere.

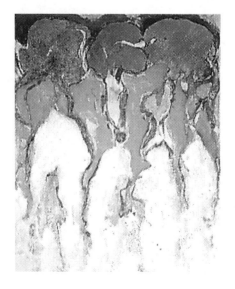

Figure 53: "Tierra No. 6," color
monoprint and gold leaf, 22" x 18," 1996.

Cochiti Gold

Numberless, numberless
yellow leaves fluttering all over the earth.
This glowing, golden bough—*it* knows.
I wander aimlessly with credulous infant eyes.
Amazing! Marvelous!
Nothing remains the same, as bright sun
burns away morning mist.

Figure 54: "Red Pine,"
dry color pastel, 17.5" x 13," 1989.

Flash

clear pond vague fish shapes
cold spring-fed bottomless dark
gold flash, dazzling void

Ode to a Chocolate Cookie

The recipe for this round blessing
combines butter, nuts and chocolate
to unleash a heavenly explosion
like combining cookie matter and anti-matter.

The lumps of nut, the small dark pools of chocolate
reveal, yet hide, the biochemistry within;
only my watering mouth, my salivating tongue can
decode the complex organic linkages.

Different neural pathways carry
dendritic signals of the chocolate, nuts and butter
from different tasters on the tongue
especially in back
to diverse centers of delectation
in my brain
and then, back—for more—to the
yearning salivation beneath
my squirming tongue.

But exactly what is happening
cannot be known.
No formula can explain.
No science knows enough to parse
the divinity of this cookie.

Chocolate molecules excite
somewhere a synapse
that says, "Oh, oh! My God!
Send more!"
The flavor of the nuts provokes

yet another song, while
the butter taste conducts the entire
chocolate chamber orchestra.

Paying homage to painter Joseph Albers
I've become a color theorist of cocoa—
discovering its pulsing complements and
reaffirming the truth of glowing
chocolate color lights.

Figure 55: "Elephant's Head," oil on linen, 24" x 30," 1990.

Figure 56: "Lake Champlain," india ink, notebook sketch, 1986.

Circus

Awakening, I see the shades of others stir.
I see what isn't there.
You are not there, nor I.
Leaves rustle, marking time.

Put aside what you know;
don't favor what is beautiful.
Just see what is there.
See with your peripheral vision
the blur that dissolves
when you look directly.

One must slow down to see
the creatures who fade at dawn.
If you rush, they dash off
like frightened fawns.

Study the bark of a ponderosa
vanilla microcosm of an
endless vertical world
ragged black cracks of time
splitting the years of rosy tan.

Don't leave!
Rushing off to the next intention
        next plan
                next hope
                        next ambition;
you will miss the circus that's in town
playing just for you.

Figure 57: "Sumacs," oil on canvas, 32" x 38." 1990.

Dorland Glimpses

Spring has come while I've been writing about the darkness.
Trees by the pond now wear a sage veil
fragrant white lilacs dot the mountainside.
At day's end, yellow-green hills ripple far off
grasses glow in the sunset.

Climbing the impassable road to my cabin
I see the geology of these mountains
working. After each rain
the rivulets deepen.
The planet's gravity is revealed by their essential straightness
steep ribbons of sand.

The bobcat is still as a stump, maybe a hundred feet away.
Liquid haunches moving a few inches each step
hugging the ground.
She moves warily toward me.
I see through her eyes; she through mine.
Then, casually, the connection is gone.
I am demoted.
Ambling off, she disappears in the brush.

I am filled with this place.
Sun glistening on myriad live oak leaves
I step out early one morning to locate
the Canadian geese honking far overhead.
But my aural compass gives false readings.
Interference from valley traffic far below
prevents a simple spring navigation.
They are lost.

When the rains come, they lash my perch.
Wind-driven drops fill the cabin space
with an angry hiss.
After awhile they relent for moments, and
as the storm spends itself
they forget, and go east.

Sometimes, like this morning, cold blustery air
moves in afterwards
ruffling the oaks.
The sun breaks through in patches.
My fire dies to coals.
Smoke drifts through sunlit leaves.
It is time to move on.

Figure 58: "Shultis Brook Farm," india ink, notebook sketch, 1988.

End

Uncommon Names and References

"Netherworld"

Bodhidharma was the legendary "Chinese patriarch of Zen," who is said to have brought Zen from India to China in the 6th Century CE. Legend also has it that, Eka, his first disciple in China, cut off his arm to show his earnest desperation to know the truth.

Kwan Yin is the legendary Chinese goddess of compassion and fertility, who evolved historically from Avalokiteshvara, the Indian bodhisattva of compassion. A bodhisattva in Zen is one who forgoes their own ultimate experience of Nirvana in order first to liberate all other suffering "sentient beings."

"Wild Flower"

Zen Master Eihei Dogen, author of the poem's epigraph, brought what came to be known as the Soto School of Zen to Japan from China in the 13th Century.

"Raven Dies and Returns to Talk"

Ikkyu, author of the poem's epigraph, was a renowned 15th Century Japanese Zen poet.

"Live Ruins"

The phrase "pueblo T's" refers to the inverted-T shape of doorways in many southwestern pueblo ruins.

"Lost Page from a Book of Hours"

Hakuin was a famous 18th Century Japanese Zen Master in the Rinzai sect of Zen.

"Cochiti Gold"

"Cochiti" is the name of a Native American Pueblo northwest of Albuquerque, and of a mountain canyon above the Pueblo.

"Ode to a Chocolate Cookie"

Joseph Albers was a renowned artist, teacher and color theorist in the famous 20th Century German Bauhaus School. He emigrated to the United States after the Nazi's closure of the Bauhaus.

"Color light" refers to the luminous effect that sometimes results from placing three colors immediately next to each other so that each one is touching both of the others – as though light were being generated from within the pigments themselves. Influenced by the work of such color theorists as Joseph Albers and Johannes Itten, such color effects were of great interest to the Bauhaus artists.

"Dorland Glimpses"

"Dorland" refers to the Dorland Art Colony near Temecula, California.

Acknowledgements

My thanks must begin with The Live Poets Society of Santa Fe, founded by friend and poet Richard Brandt. All of the members and participants in this poetry reading group deserve my gratitude as well, for all have offered comments and suggestions at numerous readings. Particular thanks go to Victor Di Suvero, who offered encouragement for assembling this volume.

Members of several other poetry reading groups also offered feedback and supported my writing efforts, including the "Eldorado Poets" in Santa Fe, and the "Nuclear Poets" in Los Alamos. I wish to extend specific thanks also to a number of people— many being writers themselves— who have read or listened to many of the poems; they include Sean Murphy, Susan Hazen-Hammond, Joan Mitchell, Frank Moore, Mary Cost, Don Levering, Judy Yarnall, Anami Curlin, Jane Lin, and Joan Logghe. All offered valued comments and suggestions.

Whatever shortcomings are found in the book are, of course, my responsibility alone.

The poem "Moon-Faced Buddha" was originally published in *Santa Fe Literary Review*, 2009.

List of Images

COVER: "Canyon Trees," oil on canvas, 28" x 22," 1998.

"Tree Line," oil on linen, 24" x 30," 1990.

"Portrait of the Artist's Father," Ross Lee Finney, charcoal, 12" x 9," 1980; digitally superimposed on musical score by RLF.

"Self Portrait," india ink, 12.5" x 9.5," 1980.

"Seashore Rocks," charcoal, 17" x 13.5," 1983.

"Way Marker No. 3," dry color pastel, 21" x 14," 1988, in collection of Pat Sampson.

"Basho Pond," 35mm color photograph, 1987.

"Monterey Surf," digital camera image, 1997.

"El Castillo del Rey (Tulum)," india ink, 9" x 12," 1988.

My older brother, Ross L. Finney, 35mm color photograph, 1998.

Me and my older brother, photograph taken by my father, 1938, in Menton, France.

"Pacific Grove Surf," charcoal, 14" x 17," 1994.

"Stump Abstraction," digital version of 35mm color photograph, 1992.

"Winter Window," 35mm color photograph, 1988.

My son Christopher, 35mm color photograph, 1996.

"Dragon Fly," india ink, 6" x 6," 1979.

"Pine Bough," india ink, notebook sketch, 1988.

"Fire," monoprint, 13.5" x 11," 1998.

"Leaf," india ink, notebook sketch, 1987.

"Uinta Mountain Cliff," charcoal, 19" x 24," 1979.

"Totem," lithograph, 15.5" x 15.5," 1994.

"Organic Forms Still Life," charcoal and conté crayon, 18" x 23," 1989.

"Vergennes," dry color pastel, 19" x 25," 1988, in the collection of Gordon Lewis, Vermont.

"Barlow's Field," dry color pastel, 12.5" x 12.5," 1988, in the collection of Lee Barlow (estate).

"Flowers," dry color pastel, 25" x 19," 1987.

"23 Bank Street," watercolor, 15" x 22," 1983.

"Barranca No. 1," oil on canvas, 30" x 30," 1995, in the collection of Haskill Rothstein, Ann Arbor, Michigan.

Family portrait in Chile, digital color photograph, 2002.

"Woods," charcoal, 14" x 17," 1998.

"Flowers," by my father, Ross Lee Finney, oil on linen, 16" x 13," n.d. (circa 1956).

"Portrait of the Artist's Father," Ross Lee Finney, dry color pastel, 20" x 17," 1986.

"Johnson Woods, Stream," india ink, 8" x 11," 1986.

"Vermont Woods," india ink, 10" x 7," 1986.

"Reclining Figures," gouache & oil stick, 15" x 19.5," 1991.

"Open Figure Gesture," gouache, 29" x 24," 1991.

"Portrait of the Artist's Mother," Gretchen Ludke Finney, charcoal, 16" x 11," 1981.

"Portrait of the Artist's Father," charcoal, 17" x 11," 1982.

"Burst," lithograph, 10" x 7," 1992.

"The Lives of Grasses," pencil, notebook sketch, 1986.

"Flower Gesture," india ink, 10" x 5," 1981.

"Tree Gesture," pencil, 15" x 14," 1979.

"Moving Figure," charcoal, 22" x 20," 1989.

"Raven Dies and Returns to Talk" (detail), mixed media on canvas, 50" x 38," 2006 (detail 23" x 38").

"Mt. Mansfield," dry color pastel, 18.5" x 24.5," 1987.

"Basalt Crystal," 35 mm color photograph, 2000.

"Pond Space," dry color pastel, 11" x 23.5," 1990.

"Barranca Study No. 3," gouache, 5.5" x 7.5," 1996, in the collection of Shelby Redondo, Los Alamos, New Mexico.

"Cottonwoods," dry color pastel, 17" x 14," 1995.

"Temporal Canyon Veil," 35mm color photograph, 1995.

"Canyon Veil," oil on linen, 40" x 50," 2008.

"Witness," photo-etching with aquatint, from a 1966 drawing, 16.5" x 13.5," 1992.

"Nude Gesture," pencil, 12" x 9," 1991.

"Calligraphic Gesture," india ink, 30" x 22," 1991.

"Embracing Figures," color monoprint, 13.5" x 11," 1998; included in 8th Annual FOCA Exhibition, Lewallen Contemporary, Santa Fe, 2005; juried by Elizabeth Smith, Chief Curator, Museum of Contemporary Art, Chicago.

"Tierra No. 6," color monoprint with gold leaf, 22" x 18," 1996.

"Red Pine," dry color pastel, 17.5" x 13," 1989, in collection of Mrs. Stanley Fischer, Illinois.

"Elephant's Head," oil on linen, 24" x 30," 1990.

"Lake Champlain," india ink, notebook sketch, 1986.

"Sumacs," oil on canvas, 32" x 38," 1990.

"Shultis Brook Farm," india ink, notebook sketch, 1988.

About The Author

Henry C. Finney is a sociologist, writer, poet, painter, meditation instructor, and senior Zen practitioner. He holds a B.A. in anthropology from the University of Michigan in Ann Arbor, a Ph.D. in sociology from the University of California at Berkeley, and an MFA in painting from Pratt Institute in New York City. He taught sociology and later art at the University of Vermont for over twenty years, during which time he published numerous professional articles and essays. He retired in 1994 to become a full-time writer and artist.

His art has been represented by Santa Fe Contemporary Art in Santa Fe, and is found in many private collections around the country. His poems have appeared in several volumes by the Santa Fe Live Poets Society, and in several poetry journals, including the *Santa Fe Literary Review*.

Mr. Finney currently lives and works in Los Alamos, New Mexico, where he runs the Kannon Zendo. More information, along with research articles, essays, poems, and art images, may be found at www.kannonzendo.org and www.hcfinneystudios.com, as well as on Facebook. Most of the art works listed there, along with many in the present volume, are available for purchase. Contact with the author may be made through these sites.